THE LITTLE BOOK OF
BEYONCÉ

Published by Orange Hippo!
20 Mortimer Street
London W1T 3JW

Copyright © 2019 Orange Hippo!
All rights reserved. No part of this publication may be reproduced,
stored in a retrieval system, or transmitted in any form or by any means
(including electronic, mechanical, photocopying, recording, or otherwise)
without prior written permission from the publisher.

ISBN 978-1-78739-375-2
Compiled by: Malcolm Croft
Project Editor: Ross Hamilton
Design: Russell Knowles, Luana Gobbo
Production: Rachel Burgess
A CIP catalogue for this book is available from the British Library
Printed in Dubai
10 9 8 7 6 5 4 3 2 1

Jacket cover photograph: Getty Images

THE LITTLE BOOK OF
BEYONCÉ

WORDS OF WISDOM FROM
QUEEN BEY

CONTENTS

INTRODUCTION

Beyoncé Knowles-Carter is, without a doubt, the most powerful musician in the world. Her first band, Destiny's Child, has become known as more of a self-fulfilling prophecy than a pop group, a proving ground for the super-ambitious singer – she created the group when she was just nine years old! – to rise not only to a position to change the world… but to run it.

Ever since DC split in the early 2000s, Planet Earth has been on bended knee in nothing but adoration for its Queen Bey. Today, she is no longer just a singer from a girl group. She is a multi-hyphenated polymath: a businesswoman-mogul-actor-brand-mother-role model. In short, she is a titan of popular culture, an icon, a legend, a superstar. Honestly, at this point, you could throw any superlative at her and it would stick.

Despite being notoriously private about her personal life and reluctant to do interviews, when Beyoncé does speak she is a quote machine, weighing in on everything from feminism, to fame, to food that is fried; when Beyoncé speaks, the world listens. It has no choice.

This Little Book of Beyoncé, therefore, is not just a tiny tome of quotes – it's also Beyoncé's guide on how to live your best life, as inspirational and aspirational as any self-help book (but a lot cheaper!). "Being an icon is my dream," she once said on stage in 2011. Imagine anyone else saying that? They'd be laughed off stage in a second. And yet, for Beyoncé, that sentence feels like an understatement. For she is so much more than even an icon… she is the world's greatest living monongm: Beyoncé.

Don't even try imagine the world without her. It just wouldn't compare. God save the Queen.

CHAPTER

ONE

DESTINY'S
CHILD

She about to steam. Stand back.

Jay-Z, 'Déjà Vu,' 2006, about Beyoncé

Whenever I'm confused about something I ask God to reveal the answers to my questions, and he does. That's how we found our name – we opened up the Bible, and the word 'destiny' was right there.

2001, about Destiny's Child

I now know that, yes, I am powerful. I'm more powerful than my mind can even digest and understand.

2013

My whole life right now feels like an endless round of promotion. I hate doing interviews, if I can be honest with you.

2004

I hate clubs. I hate the noise, I don't like the smell of smoke, I don't really even drink, and I'm not happy being the focus of everyone's attention. My, I sound like an old woman, don't I?

2004

I worked so hard during my childhood to meet this goal: By the time I was 30 years old, I could do what I want. I've reached that. I feel very fortunate to be in that position. But I've sacrificed a lot of things, and I've worked harder than probably anyone I know, at least in the music industry. So I just have to remind myself that I deserve it.

2013

"

Even now, getting covers or magazines or getting respect at labels is totally different for us, as women of colour. Even though we've sold way more records than some artists and we're way more successful, they're treated like more of a priority. I hate to say that, but it's the truth.

"

2001

I think music is something that can, and should, be used to get you into different things because eventually what goes up must come down. We're not going to be the number one group in the world forever – so you have to have something else to fall back on.

2001

The main thing I've learned is not to judge people. Because you don't really know how terrible it is to judge somebody until you get judged. And you don't know how terrible gossip is until the gossip is about you.

2001

Communication in a group is the key. We've learned about loyalty, about the importance of loving and caring about the people in the group, sticking together, how to be a friend, how to apologize when you're wrong, and how to compromise.

2001

When you love and accept yourself, when you know who really cares about you, and when you learn from your mistakes, then you stop caring about what people who don't know you think. Usually the person talking is just jealous or sad about themselves, and it takes going through this to realize that's how life is.

2001

One day, I counted the blemishes on my face. Got up to 35. It's so irritating to read in articles people saying, 'She thinks she's beautiful.' There's a lot of days that I wake up, and I hate how I look.

2001

"

I'm scared, be scared, allow it, release it, move on. **"**

2013

When we started in the '90s, R&B was the most important genre. We all kind of want that back: the feeling that music gave us.

2013

I used to start with lyrics and then I'd find tracks – often it was something I had in my head, and it just so happened to go with the melody. Now I write with other writers. It starts with the title or the concept of what I'm trying to say, and then I'll go into the booth and sing my idea. Then we work together to layer on.

2013

During my recovery [from the birth of her twins], I gave myself self-love and self-care, and I embraced being curvier. I accepted what my body wanted to be. After six months, I started preparing for Coachella. But I was patient with myself and enjoyed my fuller curves. My kids and husband did, too.

2018

I come from a lineage of broken male-female relationships, abuse of power, and mistrust. Only when I saw that clearly was I able to resolve those conflicts in my own relationship [with rapper Jay-Z]. Connecting to the past and knowing our history makes us both bruised and beautiful.

2018

I approach my shows like an athlete. It's one of the reasons I connect to the Super Bowl. You know how they sit down and watch whoever they're going to play and study themselves? That's how I treat my performances. I wish I could just enjoy them, but I see the light that was late. I see, 'Oh God, that hair did not work!'

2013

"

I love my job, but it's more than that:
I *need* it.

"

2013

Before I gave birth to [daughter] Blue Ivy, that was the only time in my life, all throughout my life, that I was lost. **"**

2013

When I'm onstage, I don't know what the crap happens. I am gone. It's like a blackout.

2013

The beauty of social media is it's completely democratic. Everyone has a say. Everyone's voice counts, and everyone has a chance to paint the world from their own perspective.

2018

My mother taught me the importance not just of being seen but of seeing myself.

2018

I will continue to explore every inch of my soul and every part of my artistry.

2018

"

I feel like my job in the industry is to push the limits, and I have to constantly evolve. **"**

2011

I'm attracted to songs that will become a dinner conversation! With 'Single Ladies' clearly I'd just gotten married, and people want to get married every day.

2011

"

'Crazy in Love' was another one of those classic moments in pop culture that none of us expected. I asked Jay to get on the song the night before I had to turn my album in – thank God he did. It still never gets old, no matter how many times I sing it.

"

2011

I can never be safe; I always try and go against the grain. As soon as I accomplish one thing, I just set a higher goal. That's how I've gotten to where I am.

2011

We all have special numbers in our lives, and 4 is that for me. It's the day I was born. My mother's birthday, and a lot of my friends' birthdays, are on the fourth; April 4 is my wedding date.

2011

Power means happiness, power means hard work and sacrifice. To me, it's about setting a good example, and not abusing your power! You still have to have humility: I've seen how you can lead by example, and not by fear.

2011

CHAPTER

TWO

INDEPENDENT
WOMAN

"

I'm like a sponge and soak everything up.

2011

At this point, I really know who I am, and don't feel like I have to put myself in a box. I'm not afraid of taking risks – no one can define me.

2011

If everything was perfect, you would never learn and you would never grow.

2013

I've fallen quite a few times, so I've learnt how to fall. It's very rare that I'm not bruised in my life. I'm always bruised somewhere — like my legs, my hips…

2013

"

I don't like to gamble, but if there is one thing I'm willing to bet on it is myself.

"

2009

Whenever I've had a video that's great, I've definitely bled somewhere – the dancing, and the shoes, and the costumes – it's always a ring or something that slices me. But you've already started so you've just gotta fight through it. ""

2013

I don't feel the pain on stage. The adrenaline takes over. But when I get off the stage? They come off.

On famously dancing in high heels
2013

Why do you have to choose what type of woman you are? Why do you have to label yourself anything? I'm just a woman and I love being a woman. If you're attractive then you can't be sexy, and you can't be intelligent? What is all of that?

2013

"

I am a modern-day feminist. I do believe in equality, and that we have a way to go and it's something that's pushed aside and something that we have been conditioned to accept. But I'm happily married. I love my husband.

"

2013

I feel like Mrs Carter is who I am, but I am more bold and more fearless than I've ever been.

2013

"

On stage, I can say anything, I can be goofy, sexy, anything that I feel.

2013

After the Super Bowl, I took a week and I ate everything I wanted to. From doughnuts to cheeseburgers to fried fish – I even had fried alligator. Anything fried.

2013

As long as I could sing, I would be happy. It just feels good to my body.

2013

Everyone in my life serves a different purpose and has a different ear, and a different type of advice. But I have to make the decisions.

2013

I'm not just self-critical. I'm critical. I'm not so critical that I don't understand what's great and what's not, but I do push people. I push them and I push myself. It's just who I am. I was that way when I was nine years old. And no one taught me that, it's just who I was.

2013

I definitely want my daughter to have goals and drive and passion — but it has to be a balance. Whatever makes her happy, I'm there.

2013

We all have our imperfections. But I'm human, and you know, it's important to concentrate on other qualities besides outer beauty.

2013

We were really sheltered. After the show we would get on the tour bus and read the Bible.

On touring with Destiny's Child, 2008

There are a lot of things I never did [while touring] because I believe in watching those true Hollywood stories and I see how easy it is to lose track of your life. Think about Marilyn Monroe.

2008

I grew up upper-class. Private school. My dad had a Jaguar. We're African-American and we work together as a family, so people assume we're like the Jacksons. But I didn't have parents using me to get out of a bad situation.

2008

I taught my girls to pick up their own suitcases. Pretty is as pretty does. Like my mother said, 'You got to be cute on the inside'.

Tina Knowles, 2008

The trick to love is to find somebody who makes you a better person. You are who you're around. And if I don't want to be like you, I don't want to be around you.

2008

"

I'm not bossy. I'm the boss.

2011

"

I put a lot of thought into how I wanted to unveil my pregnancy. It was important to me that I was able to do it myself. I decided to say nothing and proudly show my baby bump. I felt it was more powerful to see the love and enthusiasm as opposed to saying anything. **"**

2011

"

I have been pregnant through every major event I've done, from the Billboard Awards to Glastonbury.

"

2011

If you want to see the Third Ward Texas come out in me, disrespect my sister, and I will go completely crazy on you.

2011

"

It was important to me that I gave myself time to focus on becoming the woman I want to be, building my empire, my relationship, and my self-worth, before I became a mother.

"

2011

"

The best thing about marriage is the amount of growth you have because you can no longer hide from your fears and insecurities. There's someone right there calling you out on your flaws and building you up when you need the support. If you are with the right person, it brings out the best version of you.

2011

"

I am finally at the stage in my life where I am not so concerned with other people's opinions about my life decisions. It is so liberating to really know what I want, what truly makes me happy, what I will not tolerate. I have learned that it is no one else's job to take care of me but me.

"

2011

I'm thankful for my life, I'm thankful for my health and my family and for music and for having the best job in the world.

2009

When I work, I don't eat. I don't use the restroom. And I think my team is just as crazy as I am because they are right there with me pushing it and pushing themselves. **"**

2009

People don't know that these songs meant more than just the songs that are catchy. It's my life. 99

2009

My whole objective here is for people to see what they don't get to see. Just give me my band, give me a stage, some cool smoke and lights and you see the sweat, you see the pain, you see the love, you see the soul and it's about music.

2009

There's an actual story behind all of my songs and why I wrote those songs. A lot of the people in the audience would know 'Crazy in Love,' but would not particularly know this is when I met my first love ... my husband.

2009

I always will believe in the strength we have as women. And there are certain things you should not put up with and you have the choice to set the standards.

2009

There would definitely not be a Beyoncé without Destiny's Child. I love my girls.

2009

I don't need Sasha Fierce so much anymore because these days I know who I am.

2010

I don't like too much structure. I like to be free. I'm not alive unless I am creating something. I'm not happy if I'm not creating, if I'm not dreaming, if I'm not creating a dream and making it into something real. I'm not happy if I'm not improving, evolving, moving forward, inspiring, teaching, and learning.

2018

For me, balance is always really hard to find. I love so many different things, and to have the discipline to turn certain things away and focus on one thing at a time so that I can give it 100 per cent is really hard.

2010

I think a beautiful woman is someone who is confident but not competitive with other women — someone who is warm to everyone. Because my mother told me ever since I can remember that beauty is from within, that looks will fade, I have always been aware that you have to have something deeper to be really beautiful.

2010

I think we learn a lot from our female friends — female friendship is very, very important. It's good to support each other and I do try to put that message in my music.

2010

I'm never satisfied. I'm sure sometimes it's not easy working for me. I've never met anyone that works harder than me in my industry.

2009

I've worked too hard and sacrificed too much to do something silly that would mess up the brand I've created all of these years.

2009

Just because you're a celebrity, people feel like they have to know everything about you. I disagree.

2009

"

Right now, the tabloids are saying I'm pregnant, and they're naming the baby. It's hilarious. I don't know when I'll want to get married. I never pictured myself as a bride, but after my sister's wedding, I did start thinking about what kind of wedding I'd want. I don't think I want a big one. **"**

2006

We decide everything together. My word is my word. What Jay and I have is real. It's not about interviews or getting the right photo op. It's real. **99**

2008

THREE

QUEEN BEY

"

When I was little, my head was smaller and I looked like I had big Dumbo ears. I still do not wear my ears out, and that's why I wear big earrings, because they camouflage your ears. **"**

2001

My life is perfect now. People want to read about us and the old members, and how we didn't get along. Who cares? It's done. We do get along, we do love each other and support each other.

2001

I've learnt a lot about how things work. The music business is a lot like any other business; there's a lot of politics involved, it feels like people who are aggressive and mean always get credit for stuff and that nice people never do. Except the nice people always win out in the end.

1999

It's kind of hard being managed by your dad, but I know he's working extra-hard because he's going to want to make sure his babies succeed.

1999

It took Destiny's Child nine years to get on MTV.

2001

People have tried to get us into bathing suits, but there's a line we draw. We wear nothin' with our butt cheeks out, our boobs out. We like sexy clothes, but still classy. Not so people can say, 'How can they wear that and be a Christian?'

2001

I'd like to be like Barbra Streisand, doing concerts whenever I want. Sometimes I think that after a while I'm going to move away and sing in a bar somewhere, because I am a little afraid of being *too* famous.

2002

If you see me on TV, I'm not a humble, shy person, but it's a transformation into that. It's a job. In real life I'm not like that.

2002

I always held back in Destiny's Child, because I was comfortable in a group and felt that I didn't have to do anything 100 per cent, because there were other people onstage with me. **"**

2005

I never really told anybody who I really am. I battle with it, because at the end of the day, my life and my family are so much more important than any of this.

2013

"

I need to be able to go places and have normal conversations with people. You don't have to alienate yourself from the world. **"**

2013

I think about Madonna and how she started the label and developed other artists. There are not enough of those women.

2013

66

In the end I became a mother,
which is the biggest accomplishment
of my life.

99

2013

The woman who gave us our record deal, I met her when I was ten, when Destiny's Child auditioned for Columbia Records. **"**

2013

"

In this industry, the biggest mistake is not being in your right mind, and then not making the right judgement.

"

2013

I feel like my father taught me so much, and he prepared me for this. I always ran my stuff, since we were 15 years old. Now I'm controlling my content, controlling my brand and archiving it for my daughter and making sure she has it and she respects it.

2013

You see Puffy and you see my husband and you see these male artists that become moguls, and the female artists might become legends, but there's not enough of us that become moguls. **""**

2013

People don't understand the amount of studying and research that goes into greatness. But I absolutely understand it. **"**

2013

"

I don't really have to do anything
that I don't want to do anymore.
And that feels damn good.
"

2013

Light some candles, have a good meal, and watch an old movie. I don't cook much, but I'm good at spaghetti and sandwiches. I know they're easy, but they're my specialty.

On her perfect night in, 2006

"

You definitely feed off the people around you, and your man is one of the people you talk to the most. So you kind of help each other and keep each other strong. It's important. **"**

2006

My mother was such a great mother and is still such a big part of my life. I want my kids to feel that way about me. I want to be in their lives. I don't want to be away a lot, so I'm sure I'll slow down. But there are so many amazing people who do both.

2006

"

Motherhood is not as glamorous as I make it look.

,,

2006

I took a risk with acting. It was scary because it was different for me. You just always have to take risks. I always go with my gut, and it's always right. People are scared to do that.

2006

In my 'Crazy in Love' video, I was dancing so hard that my whole dress completely fell off in front of all these men.

2006

It gets easier to be confident about my body as I get older. I realize who I am, and I deal with it. I'm still kind of embarrassed that I wrote 'Bootylicious'. I had gained a little weight, and I was making fun of it. It's a silly song, but it's nice because it's made curvy women feel sexy.

2006

"

If I have a day off, sometimes I'll stay in bed all day and watch TV and eat whatever I want. I'll eat cereal and Oreos and change channels every three minutes.

"

2006

I needed a break. I needed my dad.
I had to let go.

**On separating from her manager,
and father, Matthew Knowles, 2011**

I love my husband, but it is nothing like a conversation with a woman that understands you. I grow so much from those conversations.

2011

It's difficult being a woman. It's so much pressure, and we need that support sometimes. We're all going through our problems, but we all have the same insecurities and we all have the same abilities and we all need each other.

2011

"

It's every woman's dream to feel this way about someone. **"**

About her husband, Jay-Z, 2011

I'm like most women – very generous, and I'll compromise. I used to be afraid of people thinking I was difficult or too critical, and you know, I don't really care about that anymore. Be your own advocate, no matter who thinks you're 'difficult'.

2011

People call me a diva because I'm the lead singer, so they think I'm a diva and go around kicking people out of the group. **"**

2001

I was always really quiet and shy, but I felt at home on stage. I felt I could step out of myself. Because I'm a very private person and I am not the type of personality that enjoys being looked at all the time. At a party I'm the one hanging back, observing other people. But on stage I felt at home.

2008

"

That is my alter ego and now she
has a last name. I have someone
else that takes over when it's time
for me to work and when I'm on
stage, this alter ego that I've created
that kind of protects me and who I
really am.

,,

**On alter-ego, Sasha Fierce,
2008**

It can be hard not to lose the plot. When magazines retouch you to make you look perfect, and you start to believe that you really look like that. And you can be rude to people and no one says anything 'cos they want their jobs. You can very easily lose perspective.

2008

I over-analyse everything. I want to be the best at everything, and maybe that's just me being an over-achiever. I just wish I was better at everything.

2008

The girls from Destiny's Child, we would put our hair on the ironing board, and iron it, which is so crazy! My mom who used to own a hair salon was like, 'We have to get you out of your own hair, because you are destroying it!'

2002

I don't want to get addicted to fame. Then when I'm no longer famous I won't know what to do, and I'll just seem desperate and lose my mind.

2004

When you work so much like we did, it's just too much. You lose touch with who you are.

2004

I worked so hard during my childhood to meet this goal: by the time I was 30 years old, I could do what I want. I've reached that. I feel very fortunate to be in that position. But I've sacrificed a lot of things, and I've worked harder than probably anyone I know, at least in the music industry. So I just have to remind myself that I deserve it.

2013

In relationships, I think a lot like a guy. If I do something wrong, I don't get emotional. I think about it, and I change it and fix it. I've always been very logical. **99**

2004

66

I remember walking out and I was scared, but when the music started, I don't know what happened. I just . . . changed.

99

On her first performance at a school talent show, 2004

I used to like when people made me mad. I'm like, 'Please piss me off before the performance.' I used to use everything.

2004

"

You know, equality is a myth, and for some reason, everyone accepts the fact that women don't make as much money as men do. I don't understand that. Why do we have to take a back seat? **"**

2013

I truly believe that women should be financially independent from their men. And let's face it, money gives men the power to run the show. It gives men the power to define value. They define what's sexy. And men define what's feminine. It's ridiculous.

2013

I would not be the woman I am if I did not go home to that man. It just gives me such a foundation. We were friends first for a year and a half before we went on any date – on the phone for a year and a half.

On courting Jay-Z, 2016

What does fear taste like? Success.
I have accomplished nothing without
a little taste of fear in my mouth.

2013

The sexiest thing about a man is someone being very smart and confident. And someone who doesn't try – just is cool and naturally sexy.

2003

I feel like if men really like you, then they'll approach you. I don't feel like you should go after a man.

2003

CHAPTER

FOUR

MRS CARTER

"

I don't feel like I have to please anyone. I feel free. I feel like I'm an adult. I'm grown. I can do what I want. I can say what I want. I can retire if I want. That's why I've worked hard.

2013

I look at the woman I was in my 20s and I see a young lady growing into confidence but intent on pleasing everyone around her. I now feel so much more beautiful, so much sexier, so much more interesting. And so much more powerful.

2018

I felt like I had been so commercially successful, but that wasn't enough. There's something really stressful about having to keep up with that. You can't express yourself. You can't grow. It is the battle of my life. So I set a goal. And my goal was independence.

2014

People see celebrities, and they have money and fame. But I'm a human being. I get scared and I get nervous just like everyone else.

2014

66

Power's not given to you. You have
to take it.

99

2014

The world will see you the way you see you and treat you the way you treat yourself.

2016

Having the power to make every final decision and being accountable for them is definitely a burden and a blessing. To me, power is making things happen without asking for permission. It's affecting the way people perceive themselves and the world around them. It's making people stand up with pride.

2016

Time is the most valuable asset you own, and you have to use it wisely. My parents taught me how to work hard and smart. Both were entrepreneurs; I watched them struggle working 18-hour days. They taught me that nothing worth having comes easily.

2016

"

My father stressed discipline and was tough with me. He pushed me to be a leader and an independent thinker. My mother loved me unconditionally, so I felt safe enough to dream. **"**

2016

I learned the importance of honouring my word and commitments from my mother. One of the best things about her is her ability to sense when I am going through a tough time. She texts me the most powerful prayers, and they always come right when I need them. I know I'm tapped into her emotional Wi-Fi.

2016

A feminist is someone who believes in equal rights for men and women. I don't understand the negative connotation of the word, or why it should exclude the opposite sex. If you are a man who believes your daughter should have the same opportunities and rights as your son, then you're a feminist.

2016

We need men and women to understand the double standards that still exist in this world, and we need to have a real conversation so we can begin to make changes. Ask anyone, man or woman, 'Do you want your daughter to have 75 cents when she deserves $1?' What do you think the answer would be?

2016

I hope I can create art that helps people heal. Art that makes people feel proud of their struggle. Everyone experiences pain, but sometimes you need to be uncomfortable to transform. Pain is not pretty, but I wasn't able to hold my daughter in my arms until I experienced the pain of childbirth!

2016

I just try to write songs that people are going to have a dialogue about. Songs that people are going to feel … at dinner, at the club. I want people to have some type of emotion.

2018

I'm not at all shy about having the freedom to wear something fashionable, or something sexy, or showing more skin. I have no problem with being whatever character I need to be. I have my limits, clearly, but I think that's the beauty of being a woman. We have so many different personalities and I love to tap into all of those.

2011

I think it's interesting because people think I'm a lot curvier than I am. I'm definitely not like what people's perception of me is. Every single day of my life somebody says, 'You're tiny!' Every day! I guess everyone else puts more focus on it than I do. **99**

2011

I would love people to stage dive at my shows. It would be great. I mean, I say that, although if it happens at Glastonbury I'll probably be like, 'Oh, um, wait a minute!'

2011

I would have never thought about doing Glastonbury if I wasn't there the night that Jay-Z played [in 2008]. I guess it's different with pop music as these songs are played at graduations and weddings. **"**

2011

I didn't even know I've had negative press in the past three months! I didn't. I think that's one of the great things about living my life with my family and my friends and the people that I respect and I love. I kind of stand away from that madness. There's always something negative about every celebrity if you're looking for it.

2011

I don't want to hear about why 'Single Ladies' or 'Crazy In Love' were so successful. I don't want to hear it. I believe that there are certain things that happen and they happen naturally.

2011

"

Being private controls your brand. It controls what you want to put out there and kind of forces people to talk about what you want them to talk about.

"

2008

My father had to fight those battles with racism. I didn't. And now I'm large enough – I'm universal – that no one's paying attention to what race I am. I've kind of proven myself. I'm past that.

2009

"

Michelle Obama told me she was very happy that her girls have someone like me to look up to ... And I'm like, 'Oh, my God'. **"**

2009

I wish there really was a Sasha Fierce, because I'd send her on the road and I would go and do the movies.

2009

I definitely make time for my life, it's the most important thing. The music and all that is very important, but I have to have inspiration.

2009

I'm an ambitious woman, and when I do anything, I do it really hard. If I work out, I work out really hard, if I love somebody, I love them all the way. I'm very loyal. I want a whole bunch of kids – but after I've got certain things out of my system first.

2009

When I'm being bad, I'm really bad! I'm talking cheese burgers, pizzas, French fries… You know I'm bad.

2009

The reality is: sometimes you lose. And you're never too good to lose. You're never too big to lose. You're never too smart to lose. It happens.

2015

I guess I am a modern-day feminist. I do believe in equality. Why do you have to choose what type of woman you are? Why do you have to label yourself anything?

2015

I'm learning how to drown out the constant noise that is such an inseparable part of my life. I don't have to prove anything to anyone, I only have to follow my heart and concentrate on what I want to say to the world. I run my world.

2015

CHAPTER

FIVE

RUN THE WORLD

We have to teach our boys the rules of equality and respect, so that as they grow up gender equality becomes a natural way of life. And we have to teach our girls that they can reach as high as humanly possible.

2015

Being a mother just gives you purpose. I realized why I was born and more than anything all of the things I want to pass onto my child, and the best way of doing that is not by preaching or telling her but showing her by example. **99**

2012

"

I felt like when I was having contractions, I envisioned my child pushing through a very heavy door. And I imagined this tiny infant doing all the work, so I couldn't think about my own pain... We were talking. I know it sounds crazy, but I felt a... *communication.*

"

2012

Out of everything I've accomplished, my proudest moment, hands down, was when I gave birth to my daughter Blue.

2012

Your self-worth is determined by you. You don't have to depend on someone telling you who you are.

2015

When I'm not feeling my best I ask myself, 'What are you gonna do about it?' I use the negativity to fuel the transformation into a better me.

2012

A true diva is graceful, and talented, and strong, and fearless and brave and someone with humility.

2015

We all have our imperfections. But I'm human, and you know, it's important to concentrate on other qualities besides outer beauty.

2015

"

We need to reshape our own perception of how we view ourselves. We have to step up as women and take the lead. **"**

2015

It is so liberating to really know what I want, what truly makes me happy, what I will not tolerate. I have learned that it is no one else's job to take care of me but me.

2015

I'm over being a pop star. I don't want to be a hot girl. I want to be iconic.

2015

I wanted to sell a million records, and I sold a million records. I wanted to go platinum; and I went platinum. I've been working non-stop since I was 15. I don't even know how to chill out.

2008

I have a lot of awards, and I have a lot of these things. And they're amazing, and I worked my ass off. I worked harder than probably everybody I know to get those things. But nothing feels like my child saying, 'Mommy!' Nothing feels like when I look my husband in the eyes.

2013

I wanted to sell a million records, I just sacrificed... life. Being able to walk down the street and being able to make mistakes and not have it recorded for ever, being able to have regular relationships and dates, just regular, normal things that people probably don't even think about. Being famous is hard.

2009

I never wanted to be famous for my personal life. I wanted to be famous for my music and my talent, and I always wished I could cut it out when I left the stage. And Jay was private before I met him. It was just who we were. Even before we were celebrities.

2009

My daughter introduced me to myself. You know, my mother and I are so close, and I always prayed that I would have that type of relationship with my daughter. And she's still a baby, but the connection I had with her when I was giving birth was something that I've never felt before.

2013

"

Giving birth was the most beautiful experience of my life. It was amazing. I felt like God was giving me a chance to assist in a miracle. You're playing a part in a much bigger show. And that's what life is. It's the greatest show on Earth. **"**

2013

Pregnancy is the most incredible gift anyone can have and I'm so happy I'm a woman. Men, I feel bad, they don't get to experience this. It's incredible.

2011

"

There are many shades on every journey. Nothing is black or white. I've been through hell and back, and I'm grateful for every scar.

"

Speaking to *Vogue*, 2018